Mountain Pine Ridge   John R. Meyer

Coastal Lagoons and Marshes   John R. Meyer

A Guide to the Frogs and Toads of Belize

John R. Meyer & Carol Farneti Foster

KRIEGER PUBLISHING COMPANY
MALABAR, FLORIDA
1996

Original Edition 1996

Printed and Published by
KRIEGER PUBLISHING COMPANY
KRIEGER DRIVE
MALABAR, FLORIDA 32950

Library of Congress Cataloging-in-Publication Data

Meyer, John R.
    A guide to the frogs and toads of Belize/John R. Meyer, Carol Farneti Foster.
       p.   cm.
    Includes bibliographical references
    ISBN 0-89464-963-9 (alk. paper)
    1. Frogs—Belize. 2. Toads—Belize.   I. Foster, Carol Farneti,
1953–   II. Title.
OL668.E2M48 1996
597.8′097282—dc20   95-30424
                                          CIP

10   9   8   7   6   5   4   3   2

Cover photo: Carol Farneti Foster

THIS BOOK IS DEDICATED TO
THE YOUNG PEOPLE OF BELIZE

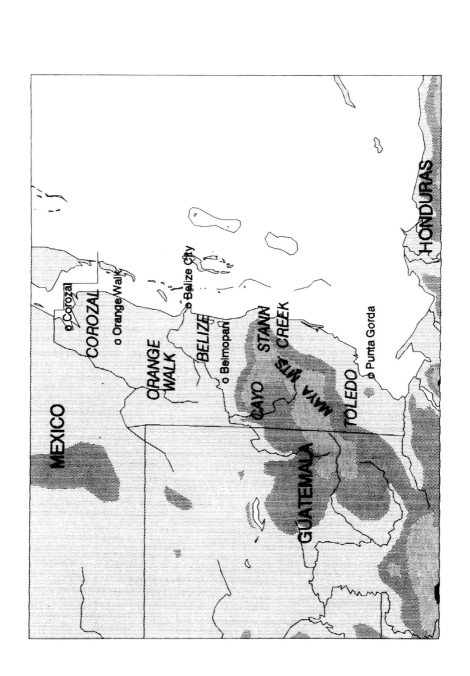

Contents

The Authors

John R. Meyer received his Ph.D. in herpetology from the University of Southern California and his B.S. and M.S. in wildlife science from Texas A&M University. He has been involved in field studies of Mexican and Central American amphibians and reptiles since 1962 and has authored several scientific papers on them, including *The Snakes of Honduras*, coauthored with Larry D. Wilson. During his two-year tenure as a lecturer in biology at the University College of Belize, Dr. Meyer and his students traveled extensively throughout Belize in the pursuit of its amphibians and reptiles, which resulted in the stimulus for the preparation of this book. He currently serves as chair of the Belize Working Group of the Declining Amphibian Populations Task Force. Dr. Meyer is an associate research scientist affiliated with Programme for Belize, and coordinator of the Navajo Natural Heritage Program in Window Rock, Arizona.

Carol Farneti Foster received her B.S. in biology from Wilkes University in Pennsylvania. She also earned a degree in medical technology and worked in tropical medicine at the University of Illinois and in ecology at the Smithsonian Institute of Tropical Research on Barro Colorado Island in Panama. While in Panama, Ms. Foster was involved in field studies on the ecology and blood parasites of anurans and iguanas. For the past ten years she has lived in Belize, making documentary films in Belize and abroad. She has a keen interest in amphibians and along with her filming career has pursued field studies of amphibians in Belize. She also serves as a member of the Belize Working Group of the Declining Amphibian Populations Task Force.

Karst Hills Forest   John R. Meyer

Interior Wetlands   John R. Meyer

Preface

With increasing recognition of Belize as a haven for the wildlife of Central America and as a destination for visitors interested in its natural beauty, it becomes obvious that Belizeans and foreigners alike are in need of printed materials to help in understanding and protecting the flora and fauna. Although a small country, Belize is extremely fortunate in having maintained its landscape in such a manner that wildlife abounds unlike any other country in the region. Among the creatures that have benefited from this wise management are the frogs and toads, collectively referred to as anurans, which have recently become the objects of concern globally, as pollution and habitat destruction are on the increase. In Belize, anuran populations continue to thrive in most areas, but long-term monitoring and vigilance will be necessary to assure their future.

With 33 species currently known from the country, Belize exhibits sufficient diversity to delight the naturalist, and its poorly known rare species continue to intrigue the professional herpetologist. At virtually any spot in the country, from the streets of Belize City to the rainforests of the Toledo District, one is never far from a frog or toad, and on almost any night, particularly rainy ones, their songs are there to enchant both visitor and resident.

This book is directed towards those Belizeans who work in natural resource management and would like to better understand the fauna, to those who see and hear these creatures daily and would like to know them better, and to the many foreign visitors and interested naturalists from other countries who appreciate the natural splendor that Belize offers. Several of the species are very poorly known and the availability of this book will assist in developing a better understanding of them. In addition to Belize, it will be useful in the Mexican states of Yucatan and Quintana Roo, and in the northern Peten region of Guatemala, as most of the wide-ranging species are shared.

The ancient Maya revered the frogs as harbingers of the life-giving rains that watered their corn, and in some areas today, modern Maya women believe that one who handles a certain frog will become a skilled tortilla maker. For some, brightly colored frogs are subjects for the camera's lens, while others are lulled to sleep by the reassuring voices of the night. Whatever their perceived value to humans may be, frogs and toads are integral parts of the natural world, and their continued presence will be an indicator of the health of the planet.

Acknowledgments

In the preparation of this book we have received frequent input from Jay M. Savage of the University of Miami. For this and his long-term moral support of Meyer's Central American endeavors, we are extremely grateful. Thanks are also extended to Roy W. McDiarmid and Louise H. Emmons, National Museum of Natural History, Washington, D.C., and to Peter Stafford, The Natural History Museum, London, for providing information on specimens and field data. We wish also to express our gratitude to Larry D. Wilson, Miami-Dade Community College, for his assistance with the literature and initial review and to Jonathan A. Campbell, University of Texas at Arlington, and Jan Meerman, Belize Tropical Forest Studies, Belize, for reading this manuscript and making helpful suggestions. Final responsibility for taxonomic judgment and errors rests with the authors, however.

In Belize, we are indebted to Sharon Matola, Belize Zoo and Tropical Education Center, for introducing Meyer to Belize and for her continuing encouragement of his work. We wish also to thank the faculty and administration of the University College of Belize for their patience and understanding during Meyer's tenure as lecturer in biology in 1992–93. At Programme for Belize, we are indebted to Joy Grant and Roger Wilson, as well as the staff of Rio Bravo field station, for their continuing support of Meyer's field studies at Rio Bravo. It has also been Meyer's pleasure to work with the staff of the Belize Audubon Society, and he is particularly grateful to Osmany Salas and the personnel of the national parks and reserves for their help and companionship in the field. Also particularly helpful during Meyer's studies in Belize were Lou Nicolait and Frances Griffith of the Belize Center for Environmental Studies, and Celeste W. Moore, Florida Game and Freshwater Fish Commission.

Among Belizean conservationists and naturalists, we are in debt to Bruce and Carolyn Miller, Wildlife Conservation International; Jan Meerman and Tineke Boomsma, Belize Tropical Forest Studies; Paul Walker,

Sarteneja; Tony Garel, Belize Zoo and Tropical Education Center; and Anelie Rodriguez, Corozal Community College for their input and field assistance. Meyer is particularly pleased to acknowledge the assistance and friendship of his many biology students at the University College of Belize, whose persistence and cheerfulness in the field was an inspiration. We would also like to express our thanks to Earl Green and Richard Belisle of the Forestry Department of the Ministry of Natural Resources for their cooperation and the assistance of field personnel under their supervision.

Thanks are also extended to the following persons for the loan of photographs used in this book: Jonathan Campbell, The University of Texas at Arlington; Courtney Conway, University of Montana; William E. Duellman, Museum of Natural History, The University of Kansas; Louise Emmons, U.S. National Museum of Natural History; John Hall, Honolulu, Hawaii; Jacob Marlin, Punta Gorda, Belize.

Finally, we would like to thank our spouses, Meyer's wife, Cyndi, and Foster's husband, Richard, for their patience and assistance in the preparation of this book and for their companionship in the field.

The Environment

TOPOGRAPHY

Although Belize lacks the high mountain ranges and intervening valleys that contribute to the biological complexity of the rest of Central America and southern Mexico, there does exist a fair degree of environmental heterogeneity within the small country. As part of the Yucatan Peninsula, which is generally flat and was frequently flooded by marine waters throughout geological history, northern Belize is primarily a limestone shelf, overlain by alluvial deposits along the major rivers. Only in the west, as one approaches the Guatemalan border, do low hills appear, with those west of the Rio Bravo escarpment, and the Yalbac Hills, reaching as high as 900 feet (300 meters) in elevation. Here in the north, major rivers such as the Rio Bravo, Booth's, Hondo, and the New River flow generally from south to north, and connect with several major wetland areas, such as New River Lagoon, Northern and Southern Lagoons, and Cox's Lagoon.

Topographically, the Belize River divides Belize in half, and to the south of the river is a region of complex physical features. The most prominent feature, occupying a large portion of the southern half of the country, is the Maya Mountains massif. The spine of the mountains runs in an arc from near Belmopan in the north, southwestward to the Guatemalan border west of Punta Gorda. The eastern slopes are relatively steep, rising from the coastal plain to elevations exceeding 3,000 feet (1,000 meters) in several places. To the west, on the leeward side, the mountains gradually descend to the Vaca Plateau, which continues on into Guatemala. At both the northern and southern extremities of the mountains are areas of karst hills, where jagged limestone is interspersed with caves, sinkholes, and underground rivers. Most of the rivers are short and swift, with those on the windward slopes, such as the Swasey and Bladen, South Stann Creek, Columbia and Rio Grande, pursuing independent courses to the Caribbean Sea. The rivers of the leeward side, such as the Raspaculo, Chiquibul, and

1

Macal Rivers, eventually join the Belize River to empty into the Caribbean. An exception just south of the Maya Divide is the Rio Machiquila, which flows westward into Guatemala to meet the Rio Usumacinta and eventually to discharge into the Gulf of Mexico.

Between the Maya Mountains and the Caribbean is a relatively flat coastal plain, which is widest in the south in the Toledo District. Most of the soils in this region are alluvium, deposited by swift streams eroding the Maya Mountains. South of Punta Gorda the low topography has encouraged the development of marshes and swamp forest, particularly along and between the Moho, Temash, and Sarstoon Rivers. In the north, between the Sibun and Mullins Rivers, and in the south around Punta Gorda, karst hills that are generally less than 300 feet (100 meters) in elevation occur almost to the edge of the sea.

CLIMATE

Lying in the tropics between 15° and 19°N latitude, Belize experiences rather uniform temperatures year round, with a mean annual temperature of 79°F (26°C), a mean high of 86°F (30°C), and a mean low temperature of 71°F (21.7°C). Winter storms from the north may bring periods of cooler and wetter weather, but temperatures never fall below the mid-40s. There are local differences due to topography, with sea level temperatures being higher than those experienced farther up in the mountains.

Climatologically, the most important factor for anurans is the seasonality and variation of precipitation in Belize. The country experiences a dry period between February and May, with the most severe effects felt in the northeast corner. Annual rainfall in Corozal is about 51 inches (1,295 mm), gradually increasing to around 65 to 70 inches (1,650 to 1,780 mm) in the central part of the country. Annual rainfall increases along the coastal plain in the south, with totals of 175 to 200 inches (4,445 to 5,080 mm) being reported in the extreme south. Rainfall is high and seasonality less severe on the eastern slopes of the Maya Mountains, while on the leeward side a rain shadow effect reduces the precipitation and seasonality is more severe.

VEGETATION

Various attempts have been made to characterize the vegetation of Belize (Russell, 1964; Neill and Allen, 1959; Hartshorn, et al., 1984; Wright, et al., 1959) depending upon the objectives of the authors. For purposes of understanding the anuran fauna of the country we are using the following simplified classification. In addition to the major types given below, each type may have a number of habitats that could be described, but this is beyond the scope of this work.

Evergreen Broadleaf Forest

This vegetation type includes the "rainforest" (in part) of Neill and Allen (1959) and the "rainforest" and "tall humid forest" of Russell (1964), and is encompassed by the Tropical Moist, Tropical Wet, Subtropical Wet, and Subtropical Lower Montane ecological formations of Hartshorn, et al. (1984). It is restricted to the southern half of the country, covering the forested coastal lowlands and the lower slopes of the Maya Mountains. Although there is a noticeable seasonality to the rainfall, the forest does not take on a dry aspect. Canopy trees are large, often approaching 100 feet (33 meters), and many possess buttress roots and are covered with epiphytes, especially bromeliads, which are important anuran shelters.

Semi-evergreen Seasonal Forest

A drier variant of the previous vegetation type, this includes the "rainforest" (in part) of Neill and Allen (1959) and the "tall moist forest" of Russell (1964), and is encompassed by the Subtropical Moist ecological formation of Hartshorn, et al. (1984). This vegetation type is extensively distributed in the northern half of the country, and extends southwestward along the Guatemalan border on the leeward side of the Maya Mountains. Its character changes from the northeast corner of the country, where the dry season is severe and many trees lose their leaves, to the forests of the Rio Bravo escarpment which exhibit a lesser degree of leaf loss. The vegetation type also appears scattered throughout the savanna wherever edaphic conditions permit, as well as along most of the streams and lagoons in the north. Many of the same tree species that occur in the Evergreen Broadleaf Forest are found in this formation, although they are generally not as tall nor as covered with epiphytes. Due to the pronounced dry season, the forest leaf litter may become dry and inhospitable to anurans.

Karst Hills Forest

Although this vegetation type has much in common with the Semi-evergreen Seasonal Forest, particularly with respect to some of the tree species and seasonal leaf loss, it owes its nature more to the underlying rock porosity than to seasonal rainfall. The Karst Hills Forest vegetation type is encompassed by the Tropical Moist Forest and Subtropical Wet Forest ecological formations of Hartshorn, et al. (1984). The vegetation type is most noticeable in the region between the Sibun and Mullins Rivers, but similar conditions may also exist in the karst hills in the Toledo District, although the higher rainfall in the south appears to mitigate against desiccation of the forest here. The Karst Hills Forest trees do not reach the heights encountered in the previous two vegetation types, buttress roots are less developed, and epiphytic growth is variable. Because of the chaotic nature of the weathered limestone, the forest floor provides terrestrial anurans with abundant shelter, as do the caves that abound in this formation.

Subtropical Evergreen Forest

This is one of the biologically least explored formations in Belize, occurring only between 1,500 and 3,000 feet (500 to 1,000 meters) in elevation on the windward slopes of the Maya Mountains. This vegetation type includes the "rainforest" (in part) and "palm brake" of Neill and Allen (1959), the "rainforest" (in part) of Russell (1964), and is encompassed within the Subtropical Lower Montane Wet Forest ecological formation of Hartshorn, et al. (1984). Because of the higher elevations, evapotranspiration is lower and moisture condensation is higher, resulting in a more humid environment and a more exuberant vegetation. The effects of the dry season are minimal, and more abundant epiphytic growth provides a variety of microhabitats for anurans. Trees are large, the canopy often reaching or exceeding 100 feet (33 meters), buttress roots are common, and the forest leaf litter is always moist, providing shelter for ground-dwelling anurans. In Belize this is the vegetation type closest to what is called "cloud forest" in Central America, and in fact it has been found to harbor what are montane forest anuran species in these other areas.

Elfin Forest

This vegetation type was termed the "elfin woodland" by Russell (1964), who encountered it on the windward slopes of the Maya Mountains above 2,600 feet (865 meters) in elevation. It is characterized by stunted trees, covered with mosses and ferns, and is frequently enveloped in clouds. The tree roots and spaces between rocks are filled with humus, mosses, ferns, and other small plants. There is very little known of the anuran inhabitants of this formation, and no species are known to be restricted to it.

Savanna

This is an extensive vegetation type in northern, central, and coastal southern Belize, and was termed the "palm and pine savanna" by Neill and Allen (1959) and the "pine savanna," "pine ridge," and "broken pine ridge" by Russell (1964). It is encompassed within the Subtropical Moist Forest and Tropical Moist Forest ecological formations of Hartshorn, et al. (1984). The essential nature of this vegetation type is its openness, tempered by a variety of tree and shrub associations. The predominant plants are grasses and sedges, with stands of pines, oaks, palms, and a variety of shrubby trees in places. This formation owes its existence to edaphic factors, drying to rock hardness during the dry season, and frequently flooding during the rainy season. A noticeable feature of the savannas is the presence of fires, both natural and human induced, during the dry season. Temporary ponds, marshes, and streams are common, providing abundant rainy season breeding places for adaptable anurans. Savannas are found extensively west of the Northern Highway, along both sides of the Western Highway in the Belize District, and along the Coastal and Southern Highways between the Sibun and Deep Rivers.

Mountain Pine Ridge

This vegetation type is somewhat of an anomaly, surrounded as it is by broadleaf forest. It was termed "pine parkland" by Neill and Allen (1959) and "pine forest" by Russell (1964), and lies within the Subtropical Moist Forest ecological formation of Hartshorn, et al. (1984). In appearance it differs little from the pine savannas of lower elevations, but it may owe its existence to the erosion of marine sediments to expose a core of Paleozoic crystalline rock or metasediments. To some extent, the savanna-like vegetation is also determined by frequently occurring fires. Situated on the northwestern corner of the Maya Mountains, the Mountain Pine Ridge is dissected by numerous swiftly flowing streams that are bordered by broadleaf evergreen vegetation. For anuran species these latter habitats are important, resulting in a fauna that differs to some degree from the pine savannas found elsewhere in Belize.

Interior Wetlands

This vegetation type is found throughout the lowlands of Belize, and was termed "fresh-water savanna" by Russell (1964), and is encompassed by the Subtropical Moist Forest, Tropical Moist Forest, Subtropical Wet Forest, and Tropical Wet Forest ecological formations of Hartshorn, et al.

(1984). Wetland situations, varying from swamps and marshes to extensive freshwater lagoons, are prominent in the northern part of the country, and a few extensive swamps are to be encountered in the Toledo District. Surrounding vegetation can consist primarily of grasses, sedges, and rushes, or may be more complex with extensive palm and hardwood forests. This formation is particularly important for anurans, as it generally remains wet throughout the year.

Coastal Lagoons and Marshes

In certain coastal areas of Belize, this vegetation type forms extensive stands. It was termed the "red mangrove swamp" and "black mangrove forest" by Neill and Allen (1959), and the "red mangrove" and "brackish savanna" by Russell (1964). The primary influence is that of the marine environment, with some areas being covered by mangroves and others by coastal wetlands of varying degrees of salinity. In general, this is a hostile environment for most anurans, although some of the widespread species may be encountered in some situations.

Anuran Biology

Belize's frogs and toads, as amphibians, are typically tied to both the terrestrial and aquatic environments. The majority of the species depend completely upon the aquatic environment for at least the larval stage of their life, and those that don't are still dependent upon the availability of moisture. Among the 33 species representing 7 families of anurans, there are a wide range of lifestyles to be found. Many are terrestrial in the adult stage, while an equal number are primarily arboreal, and a few are fossorial. All, however, have adapted in one way or another to deal with the seasonality of moisture availability in most of Belize, and these adaptations are reflected in the apparent scarcity or abundance of these creatures at different times of the year.

All of Belize's anurans are carnivorous in their feeding habits as adults, with insects and other arthropods forming most of the diets. The vast size differences among the frogs and toads, ranging from an ounce or two to as much as three pounds, ensures that prey species of all sizes are taken. Some large species, such as the marine toad and the rainforest frog, will undoubtedly eat small vertebrates given the chance, but for the most part, smaller prey is in order. Larval anurans, or tadpoles, feed primarily upon plant material, such as algae, but a few are known or thought to eat other frog eggs and occasionally other tadpoles.

Among anurans, one of the most important facets of their behavior, and certainly the one with which humans are most familiar, is their vocalization. Primarily a male characteristic, vocalization is important in establishing breeding territories and in attracting females in the majority of Belizean frogs and toads. Only among the genus *Eleutherodactylus*, the rainfrogs, is vocalization of diminished significance, a phenomenon that may be in some way connected with their habit of laying eggs on land away from water bodies. Among the most characteristic of the night sounds during the rainy season in Belize are the multitudes of calling frogs and toads. To the unpracticed ear it may all sound like just so much noise, but to the anurans and the discerning human listener, there is a wealth of information in the air. No two species sound the same, a factor that is of great significance in breeding congregations that may include thousands of anurans representing as many as eight or nine species. Each species responds to its own call, thus ensuring that a minimum of energy is expended in the breeding effort.

The frogs and toads have evolved a number of ways to continue the life cycle. Many species lay their eggs in the water, the male fertilizing them as the female deposits them in jelly-coated strands, clumps, or singly. Others, using their legs, utilize the jelly and other secretions to whip up a foam nest into which the eggs are deposited to complete their development on the water's surface or in holes in the ground. These latter nests are later flooded to release the tadpoles into the water. Some of the treefrogs deposit their eggs on vegetation overhanging the water, and the tadpoles fall into the water upon hatching. A few lay their eggs in water collected in arboreal bromeliads or in tree holes, where the tadpoles complete their development in relative safety. Finally, there are those frogs of the genera *Eleutherodactylus* and *Syrrhophus* that deposit their eggs in moist, secluded spots on the land, where the eggs undergo direct development into tiny froglets.

Although some of Belize's anurans breed throughout the year, for most species the time of greatest significance is the rainy season, beginning in June and lasting until November. It is during these months that the moisture-dependent anurans can be assured of an adequate supply of water at their breeding sites, and it is at these breeding sites that it is most convenient for humans to observe them. Many of the species retreat high into the forest trees or burrow beneath the ground following the breeding episodes, and their whereabouts at these times are often a mystery for human investigators. At the height of the dry season in some parts of the country it seems impossible that there could be any chance of anuran survival, but following a downpour of a few inches of rain the land comes alive with frogs and toads. These creatures, more than most, can call our attention to the rejuvenating cycles of nature.

Species Accounts

In this section, accounts of each of the 33 known species of Belizean anurans are given. It is very likely that future editions of this book will have at least a few additions to make, as more extensive field studies are undertaken, particularly in the Maya Mountains. As an example, in 1990 only 28 species were known from the country, with the additional 5 species being discovered in the Maya Mountains in the short period of 4 years.

For most of the Belizean frogs and toads there are no generally accepted common names, either in Belize or elsewhere. We have tried to use those few names that are reasonably well known, and in other cases have relied upon the recently published *Scientific and Common Names for the Amphibians and Reptiles of Mexico* (Liner, 1994). In many cases we have devised names that emphasize some outstanding feature of the animal, its habitat, or range. Because of their variability and often overlapping nature, common names occasionally in use in Belize are not utilized. The scientific names are those that are listed in *Amphibian Species of the World*, both the original (Frost, 1985) and the update (Duellman, 1993).

The species accounts are separated into six sections as follows. The metric system is not generally used in Belize, so all measurements are given in inches and feet, followed by the metric equivalents in parentheses.

Range—refers to the entire range of the species, with the elevational designations low = 0 to 1,800 feet (0 to 600 meters), moderate = 1,800 to 4,500 feet (600 to 1,500 meters), intermediate = 4,500 to 8,000 feet (1,500 to 2,700 meters).

Distribution—covers the known or suspected distribution, both elevational and geographical, in Belize. For several species, their distributions in Belize are poorly known, and one objective of this publication is to increase knowledge in this area.

Distinguishing Features—characters are given here that, along with the accompanying photos, will assist the observer in the identification of the individual species. Size is given to the nearest ¼ inch. An attempt has

9

been made to minimize the use of specialized terminology, although the user will need to have some familiarity with general anuran anatomy.

Habitat/Habits—the occurrence of each species in the vegetation formations is given here, along with any known specific habitat preference. In some cases, information on habitat preference and habits is drawn from studies in adjacent Central American countries, especially for species that are poorly known in Belize. The approximations of vocalizations are given to assist the observer, but it is very difficult to put anuran sounds into words. In this case, there is no substitute for hearing the call in the field and identifying the caller.

Breeding—information is given here on the breeding biology of the individual species as far as is known. In many cases, the information comes from studies of the anurans in other countries, although where we have specific information on Belizean populations it has been utilized.

Remarks—this section contains information on varied facets of the individual species, particularly where we wished to call special attention to a point or clarify a situation.

Krieger Publishing Company
P.O. Box 9542
Melbourne, FL 32902-9542

Name _____
Address _____
City _____ State__ Zip___

USE THIS FORM TO
REQUEST FUTURE CATALOGS

Subject Categories

(C) Medical Sciences
(D) Physical Therapy
(E) Psychology/Sociology
(F) Education/Communication
(G) Anthropology/Philosophy
(H) History/Religion
(I) Legal and Public Affairs
(J) Engineering/Technology
(K) Chemistry/Biochemistry
(L) Physics
(N) Mathematics/Statistics
(P) Business Sciences/Economics
(R) Biological Sciences
     (Botany, Ecology, Zoology, Biology, Nature)
(S) Physical Sciences
     (Geology, Geography, Oceanography, Water/Soil
     Management, Astronomy, Meteorology, Ecology,
     Environmental Science)
(T) Computer & Information Science
(U) Applied and Fine Arts
(V) Veterinary Medicine
(W) Adult Education
(X) Orbit Series
(Y) Public History
(Z) Herpetology

Send me/us lists in the following subject areas: (Please choose up to four (4) categories from those listed above.)

Please Print

Name _____

Mailing Address _____

City_____

State _____ Zip_____

All orders should be addressed as follows:

Krieger Publishing Company
P.O. Box 9542
Melbourne, FL 32902-9542
(407) 727-7270

(100M) 10/92
Long

Savanna   John R. Meyer

Savanna   John R. Meyer

JOHN MEYER

MARINE TOAD
Bufo marinus (Linnaeus)

Range:	Low and moderate elevations from Texas to Brazil on the Atlantic versant and Sinaloa, Mexico, to South America on the Pacific. Introduced into tropical and subtropical areas in many other parts of the world.
Distribution:	Common at lower elevations throughout Belize.
Distinguishing Features:	This is the largest anuran in Belize, with individuals up to 7 in (1,780 mm) in length and weighing up to 3 lb (1.3 kg). Its dry, warty skin and enlarged parotoid glands will distinguish it from all frogs in Belize, and its size and the triangular shaped parotoid gland distinguishes it from the related *Bufo campbelli* and *B. valliceps*.
Habitat/ Habits:	The marine toad inhabits a wide variety of situations, but is seldom encountered far from water. In the heavily forested regions it is usually seen along streams, while in open habitats such as the savanna, it is usually to be found around the hardwood hammocks. It is also a common inhabitant of populated areas, where it has adapted to

feeding opportunities provided by humans. These large toads will apparently eat anything of appropriate size, even learning to reach and devour food left out for dogs and cats. In spite of their size, they are surprisingly adept at climbing and jumping. They are known to prey on other anurans and reportedly mimic the calls of the tungara frog to attract them as prey during the breeding season. They are almost exclusively nocturnal, hiding under logs, boards, rocks, or thick vegetation during the day. The milky secretion of the parotoid glands is a strong irritant and is toxic to small animals, including dogs. The call is a loud rolling trill that may be heard for some distance when in chorus and has been likened to the sound of an idling diesel engine.

Breeding: In general, the marine toad may be said to be a year-round breeder, but this is tempered to some extent by local conditions. It may frequently be heard calling during the dry season, and tadpoles may be encountered in permanent water during these times. In areas where rainy season floods may scour the streams, marine toads probably breed during the dry season to escape these waters. Eggs are laid in the shallow waters of permanent ponds, streams, and freshwater lagoons, as well as in a variety of temporary situations. The eggs are laid in strings, usually attached to vegetation, and hatch after several days into small black schooling tadpoles. The tadpoles metamorphose after a few weeks into small toadlets that grow rapidly, reportedly reaching sexual maturity in about a year.

JONATHAN CAMPBELL

RAINFOREST TOAD
Bufo campbelli Mendelson

Range:	Low and moderate elevations of the Caribbean versant in Guatemala and Belize.
Distribution:	Known definitely only from the southern Maya Mountains in the Toledo District.
Distinguishing Features:	This is a medium-sized toad, resembling *Bufo valliceps* in size. In general appearance it is very similar to this species, but differs in having longer legs, a smaller tympanum, preorbital and pretympanic crests absent, smoother skin, a longer head, and the snout acutely rounded in lateral view and pointed in dorsal view.
Habitat/ Habits:	The rainforest toad appears to be an inhabitant of the primary forests, and is currently known from the Evergreen Broadleaf Forest and Subtropical Evergreen Forest formations, from between about 300 and 2,500 feet (100 and 833 meters) in elevation. Although probably primarily a nocturnal species, this toad may on occasion be encoun-

tered during the daytime on the darkened forest floor. The call has been described as a very soft trill.

Breeding: This recently recognized species is thought to breed in small mountain streams, as individuals have been observed calling and in amplexus in these situations. The breeding season in Belize is unknown, but the absence of water in some streams in the dry season may restrict breeding to the wetter months.

Remarks: The rainforest toad was first recognized as a distinct species in 1994, and several Belizean records for *Bufo valliceps* probably pertain to this species. It appears that the latter is an inhabitant of disturbed and cultivated areas, secondary growth, and some of the other less humid vegetation types in Belize, while *B. campbelli* is restricted to the areas of primary rainforest. The true extent of the distribution of *campbelli* in Belize must await re-evaluation of all populations of medium-sized toads in the forested areas of the country.

JOHN MEYER

GULF COAST TOAD
Bufo valliceps **Wiegmann**

Range: Low and moderate elevations of the Atlantic versant from the southeastern United States to Costa Rica and from the Isthmus of Tehuantepec, Mexico, to Guatemala on the Pacific.

Distribution: Common throughout Belize from sea level to at least 1,000 ft (335 m) in elevation.

Distinguishing Features: The Gulf Coast toad, a medium-sized anuran of about 4 in (100 mm) snout-vent length, can be differentiated from all the Belizean frogs by its dry, warty skin, and its prominent parotoid glands and cranial crests. From the similarly-sized *Bufo campbelli*, it differs in having shorter legs, larger tympanum, a more warty skin, preorbital and pre-tympanic crests present, and a rounded snout in dorsal view. It differs from *Bufo marinus* in its smaller body size, its much smaller parotoid gland, and in the absence of a tarsal fold. There is considerable variation in ground color, ranging from grey, to yellow, tan, brown, to orange, variants that may be in evidence in the same population.

Habitat/
Habits:

This species is one of the widest ranging amphibians in Belize, being found from sea level to moderate elevations, and inhabiting the savannas, agricultural and urban lands, and undisturbed forest. It appears to be a ubiquitous species wherever appropriate water is available for breeding at some time during the year. Except during periods of explosive breeding activity, these toads are nocturnal in most areas. They are strictly terrestrial, blending with the dead leaves of the forest floor or hiding under logs, rocks, and other debris when not active. The call of the male is a short trill, repeated frequently, and a large chorus can be quite deafening.

Breeding:

The Gulf Coast toad appears to be capable of breeding throughout the year in Belize, depending upon local conditions. In areas with a marked dry season, the first heavy rains will set off episodes of explosive breeding, with large, noisy choruses of males in evidence. Elsewhere, particularly in the wetter areas, breeding may take place at any time of the year. Eggs are deposited in ponds, lakes, temporary pools, roadside ditches, and the slower waters of streams, with the strings of eggs generally attached to vegetation. The eggs hatch in a few days to a week, and the black tadpoles metamorphose in a few weeks to become tiny patterned toadlets that blend well with the substrate.

Remarks:

The ecological relationship of the Gulf Coast toad with the recently described *Bufo campbelli* is poorly understood at this time. The latter appears to be an inhabitant of primary rainforest, while *B. valliceps* is more commonly found in disturbed situations, secondary forests, and the less humid forest formations in Belize. Re-assessment of the occurrence of these two species will be necessary before their exact distributions in Belize can be understood.

COURTNEY CONWAY

MAYA RAINFROG
Eleutherodactylus chac Savage

Range: Low and intermediate elevations of the Atlantic versant
                  from Belize and Guatemala to Honduras.

Distribution: Known only from about 300 to 3,000 ft (100 to 1,000 m) on
                  the windward slopes of the Maya Mountains in the Stann
                  Creek and Toledo Districts but probably also occurs in the
                  Cayo District.

Distinguishing This is the smallest of the Belizean rainfrog species, with a
Features: maximum snout-vent length of about 1.5 in (40 mm). It
                  differs from similarly sized species of *Leptodactylus* and
                  Rana in having slightly enlarged toe disks, a dark face
                  mask, and basal toe webbing only. It can be differentiated
                  from *Syrrhophus leprus* by its dark face mask, the alternat-
                  ing light and dark bands on the upper surfaces of the
                  limbs, and the presence of a dark triangular seat patch.
                  The species differs from the similarly sized *Eleutherodac-
                  tylus rhodopis* in having toe webbing and an inner tarsal
                  fold, both of which are lacking in the *rhodopis*. There is

some pattern variation in certain populations, with some individuals lacking the dark face mask and most dorsal markings; so far these variants have been encountered only at the higher elevations of the southern Maya Mountains. In life, the iris is red.

Habitat/ Habits: The Maya rainfrog is strictly an inhabitant of the Broadleaf Evergreen Forest and Subtropical Evergreen Forest formations of southern Belize, where it inhabits the leaf litter. It is generally active during the day, hopping in a zigzag course across the forest floor, but individuals are occasionally encountered at night. In areas where conditions are right, these small frogs may occur in surprisingly high numbers, while in other situations they may be only rarely encountered. Males are not known to vocalize.

Breeding: As with most other members of the genus, the Maya rainfrog lays encapsulated eggs out of water that hatch directly into small frogs. It is not known if there is a definite breeding season in Belize, but recently hatched froglets have been found in the southern Maya Mountains in December and March.

Remarks: This frog is named for *chac*, the Maya rain god.

LOUISE EMMONS

BROADHEAD RAINFROG
Eleutherodactylus laticeps (A. Dumeril)

Range: Low and moderate elevations of the Atlantic versant from Chiapas, Mexico, to northwestern Honduras.

Distribution: In Belize, known only from about 600 to 3,000 ft (200 to 1,000 m) in the Maya Mountains. Records are from Cayo and Toledo Districts, although it probably also occurs in Stann Creek District.

Distinguishing   This species, which may reach 3.5 in (88 mm) in snout-
Features: vent length, has only minimal toe webbing. It has a granular dorsal surface, usually a suprascapular fold, and well-developed dorsolateral glandular ridges. A dark face mask is usually present and there is no dark seat patch. The dorsal color is medium to dark brown, with a variety of lighter markings, sometimes including a mid-dorsal light stripe. The legs are banded with light and dark brown; the finger and toe disks are only slightly expanded. In life, the iris is yellow. Small *laticeps* might be confused with *E. chac*, but the latter has a dark seat patch and red iris in life.

Habitat/
Habits:

An inhabitant of the Evergreen Broadleaf Forest and Sub-tropical Evergreen Forest formations, where it has been found on the forest floor, in grass at the edge of the forest, and on a low bush at the edge of a forest clearing. The few records that are available indicate that this frog may be active during the daytime and at night, depending upon local conditions. Their pattern allows them to blend well with their forest surroundings. There is no known vocalization by this rainfrog.

Breeding:

As with most members of the genus, the broadhead rain-frog presumably lays eggs in leaf litter on the ground, and these undergo direct development into small frogs. The lack of vocalization is probably a reflection of the lack of congregation in choruses at breeding sites. A small individual has been found in December, indicating that breeding may take place during the rainy season.

Remarks:

Eleutherodactylus stantoni was described from Valentin in the Cayo District, but this name is now considered to be a synonym of *E. laticeps*.

JOHN MEYER

LIMESTONE RAINFROG
Eleutherodactylus psephosypharus Campbell, Savage, and Meyer

Range:	Low and moderate elevations of the Atlantic versant in Belize, Guatemala, and possibly Honduras.
Distribution:	Known from between 600 and 2,000 ft (200 and 667 m) in elevation in the Columbia River Forest Reserve and the Bladen Nature Reserve in the southern Maya Mountains in Belize.
Distinguishing Features:	This is another moderately large rainfrog, reaching about 2.5 in (65 mm) in snout-vent length. Dorsal ground color is medium to dark brown, with variable amounts of darker spots; no mid-dorsal light stripe is present in any known specimen. Lips and upper limb surfaces are barred, and the adpressed heels extensively overlap at the vent. The dorsal surface is very rugose, almost toadlike in appearance. Toe webbing is rudimentary, with the disks of the fingers and toes expanded, especially the two outer fingers The posterior thighs are light, with little or no dark

mottling. The iris is uniform bronze with fine black reticulations and a broad black band from the bottom of the pupil to the lower eyelid.

Habitat/
Habits:
The limestone rainfrog is known only from karst limestone outcrops in the Evergreen Broadleaf Forest and Subtropical Evergreen Forest formations of the southern Maya Mountains. Individuals have been found on the ground and limestone boulders at night and in caves and crevices in the limestone during the daytime. They have never been found near water, although they are active during rains. There is no known vocalization for this species.

Breeding:
In Guatemala, a female of this species has been found with developing eggs beneath a large rotting stump. They are thought to breed year round in Guatemala, although in the slightly drier Maya Mountains this might not be true.

Remarks:
This recently described rainfrog appears to be an inhabitant of pristine rainforest throughout its range. It differs from other members of the *Eleutherodactylus rugulosus* group in that it is usually found far from streams. The name *psephosypharus* is an allusion to the dark, tuberculate skin of the species.

JONATHAN CAMPBELL

LOWLAND RAINFROG
Eleutherodactylus rhodopis (Cope)

Range:	Low and moderate elevations of the Atlantic versant from San Luis Potosi, Mexico, to northwestern Honduras, and on the Pacific versant from Oaxaca, Mexico, to El Salvador.
Distribution:	In Belize, definitely known only from near Gallon Jug in the Orange Walk District. Probably occurs in forested areas of western Orange Walk and northwestern Cayo Districts.
Distinguishing Features:	These rainfrogs are about 1.5 in (40 mm) snout-vent length, about the same size as *Eleutherodactylus chac*, from which they differ in the lack of toe webbing and tarsal folds, and in having a bronze iris in life.
Habitat/ Habits:	Based upon the known Belizean locality and records from the adjacent Peten region of Guatemala, this frog appears to be a resident of the Semi-Evergreen Seasonal Forest formation. It is known to inhabit the leaf litter of the forest floor and during the dry season probably retreats to the

more humid habitats along streams, which possibly re-stricts its distribution to those areas with permanent water. Males apparently do not vocalize.

Breeding: The lowland rainfrog presumably breeds during the rainy season in Belize, as its distribution appears to be limited to the Semi-Evergreen Seasonal Forest formation. As with other members of the genus, encapsulated eggs are prob-ably laid in leaf litter or under rotting logs, with direct development into small frogs.

Remarks: Although fairly well known in the northern part of its range, *E. rhodopis* in Guatemala, Belize, and Honduras is poorly understood. It is surprising that it has been found only once in Belize, and that over 50 years ago, indicating that the area may represent marginal habitat for the spe-cies. It is the only member of the genus known from north of the Belize River, although it is possible that *Eleuthero-dactylus rugulosus* may eventually be found along some permanent streams in western Orange Walk and north-western Cayo Districts.

JOHN MEYER

CENTRAL AMERICAN RAINFROG
Eleutherodactylus rugulosus (Cope)

Range: Low and moderate elevations from Puebla, Mexico, on the Atlantic versant, and Oaxaca, Mexico, on the Pacific, to Panama.

Distribution: In Belize, the Central American rainfrog is known from south of the Belize River, in the Stann Creek, Cayo, and Toledo Districts, at elevations between 100 and at least 3,000 ft (33 and 1,000 m). It may also occur along streams in the forested areas of western Orange Walk District.

Distinguishing Features: A moderately large to large member of the genus, with adults reaching at least 3 in (75 mm) in snout-vent length. Fingers and toes have only rudimentary webbing, and the disks are not noticeably expanded. Dorsal color is generally medium to dark brown, with a light mid-dorsal stripe of varying width often present. Lips and upper surfaces of the limbs usually have a barred appearance. The dorsum and upper limb surfaces usually have a warty or rugose appearance. The posterior thigh is strongly mottled with a dark brown and cream pattern, and the heels of the adpressed limbs strongly overlap at the vent in adults. The upper one-third of the iris is gold, while the lower two-thirds is deep bronze with dark reticulations; the eyes shine red at night.

Habitat/
Habits:
An inhabitant of the Evergreen Broadleaf Forest and Subtropical Evergreen Forest formations of the southern half of the country. It may also occur in the hills of western Orange Walk District and northwestern Cayo District, where permanent streams flow through the Semi-evergreen Seasonal Forest formation. The Central American rainfrog is usually encountered at night along streams in the forest, although it may be found several hundred yards from streams during the daytime under humid conditions. At night, particularly during the dry season, they invariably occupy the stream banks, where they may also be encountered up to 3 ft (1 m) above ground in bushes and on tree limbs. Males of this species apparently do not vocalize.

Breeding:
The Central American rainfrog deposits it eggs under leaves and other debris on the forest floor, as is usual for frogs of the genus *Eleutherodactylus*. The breeding season is unknown in Belize, although it presumably is during the rainy season, as small individuals have been encountered from December to March.

Remarks:
The *rugulosus* species group is currently being investigated by Jonathan Campbell and Jay Savage, and future revision may result in a different name being applied to the Belizean form. At present, it appears that only one species of "*rugulosus*" occurs in Belize.

JOHN MEYER

RIVER RAINFROG
Eleutherodactylus sp.

Range: Known only from the Maya Mountains of Belize.

Distribution: In Belize, this species is known from between 500 and 1,200 ft (165 and 400 m) from the Cayo, Stann Creek, and Toledo Districts in the Maya Mountains.

Distinguishing Features: Possibly the largest of the Belizean members of the genus, the river rainfrog reaches at least 3.5 in (90 mm) snout-vent length. The dorsal ground color is olive to tannish brown, with variable darker markings; no mid-dorsal stripe is present in any known specimens. The posterior thighs are strongly mottled with a dark brown and cream pattern; the adpressed heels show little or no overlap at the vent in adults. Toes have basal webbing, and the finger and toe disks are only slightly expanded. The lips and upper limbs are banded with light and medium brown coloration. The dorsum and upper limb surfaces have a slightly warty or rugose appearance. The iris is gold to copper with fine dark reticulations; there is no division of the iris as in *E. rugulosus*, to which it appears to be related. There is no red eye shine at night.

Habitat/Habits: This species appears to be restricted to the rock ledges in certain streambeds of the windward slopes of the Maya Mountains in the Evergreen Broadleaf Forest formation. The river rainfrog is strictly nocturnal as far as is known, being found on the face of the ledges and behind water falling over the rocks. Captive females were heard to give a short explosive call that could be described as a "woof," not unlike a distant dog bark. The calls were uttered at variable intervals and were subdued. The function of this vocalization in the wild is unknown, as the frog's habitat can be quite noisy due to the falling stream waters.

Breeding: Nothing is known of the breeding habits of the river rainfrog, although it presumably lays encapsulated eggs on land as do other members of the genus. Egg laying probably takes place away from the streams, and breeding may take place during the rainy season, as less-than-half-grown individuals were encountered during December.

Remarks: This form may be the same as one with similar habits in Guatemala, but proper species allocation must await a revision now being undertaken by Jonathan Campbell of the University of Texas at Arlington. Specimens apparently representing one species are definitely known from the head of Roaring Creek in the Cayo District, and from the upper Columbia River in the southern Maya Mountains in the Toledo District. In addition, what appear to be representatives of the same species have been reported from the Cockscomb Basin and Silver Creek, along the Hummingbird Highway.

JOHN MEYER

WHITE-LIPPED FROG
Leptodactylus labialis (Cope)

Range:	Low and moderate elevations from Texas on the Atlantic versant and Guerrero, Mexico, on the Pacific to South America.
Distribution:	This species has a country-wide distribution in Belize, although it avoids the heavily forested areas.
Distinguishing Features:	The white-lipped frog is a small to moderate-sized frog, with adults reaching a snout-vent length of about 1.5 in (38 mm). The dorsal ground color is usually tan to brown, with variable dark markings; a white or cream line is present on the upper lip. Fingers and toes are not expanded to form disks. There are dorsolateral folds present and the dorsum has a slightly warty appearance. A ventral disk is present, and there is a distinct light longitudinal stripe on the posterior thigh. Males have paired, external vocal sacs and no horny spines on the thumbs.
Habitat/ Habits:	This frog nominally occurs in all the vegetation types in Belize except the Subtropical Evergreen Forest and Elfin

Forest formations. In the heavier forested areas, it is generally found in edge or cleared situations. This is a common but secretive frog, spending much of its time in holes and under logs, rocks, and other debris during the dry season. During the rainy season, males are frequently heard calling from holes at the base of clumps of grass and occasionally from the surface. The call is best described as a series of notes that sound like "wort, wort, wort." Although they may occasionally call during daylight hours, the species is primarily nocturnal.

Breeding: The white-lipped frogs deposit their eggs in a covered hole, excavated by the male, from where he vocalizes. The eggs are contained within a froth nest made by the male as the eggs are laid, and it serves to protect them from desiccation until rising waters free the tadpoles. Depending upon the size of the water body, a few males to several dozen may utilize a breeding site, frequently a temporary pond or rain-filled ditch. This is one of the first anurans to begin calling and breeding at the start of the rainy season. Because of the ephemeral nature of their breeding sites, the tadpoles usually metamorphose in less than 2 weeks.

JOHN MEYER

BLACK-BACKED FROG
Leptodactylus melanonotus (Hallowell)

Range: Low and moderate elevations from Tamaulipas, Mexico, on the Atlantic versant and southern Sonora, Mexico, on the Pacific to Ecuador.

Distribution: Found throughout the country at elevations from sea level to at least 1,000 ft (335 m) in most of the vegetation formations.

Distinguishing Features: This is a small frog, with a maximum snout-vent length a little more than 1.5 in (38 mm). The dorsal color is variable, from dark brown to light grey-brown, with scattered darker markings. A light line below the eye is present in some specimens. The fingers and toes are without webs, and they are not expanded at the tips to form disks. There are no dorsolateral glandular folds, and the skin is not noticeably warty as in *Leptodactylus labialis*. Males can also be distinguished from *labialis* by the presence of two black spines on the first finger in *melanonotus*.

Habitat/
Habits: Black-backed frogs can be found throughout Belize wherever there is permanent water that is not fast-moving. They inhabit the edges of marshes, ponds, forest pools, and slow-moving streams. They are most frequently encountered at the base of clumps of grass at the edge of the water, although during dry periods they can be found beneath logs, rocks, and other forest debris. The call of males is a rapid series of sounds described as "took, took, took."

Breeding: Breeding in most areas appears to be associated with the rainy season, although a heavy rain during the dry season may induce calling and possibly breeding. The males call from the base of clumps of grass, and the eggs are deposited in a foam mass that floats on the surface of the water. This species is commonly heard calling during the daylight hours, especially during the rainy season.

Remarks: Although the distribution of this species is well known in the lowlands, little information is available on its occurrence in the Maya Mountains, especially in the heavily forested regions.

JOHN MEYER

TUNGARA FROG
Physalaemus pustulosus (Cope)

Range:	Low and moderate elevations from Veracruz, Mexico, on the Atlantic versant and Oaxaca, Mexico, on the Pacific to South America.
Distribution:	In Belize, this species is known only from the northern half of the country, particularly the Orange Walk District between the Northern Highway and the Guatemalan border. Localities range from about 100 to 700 ft (33 to 233 m) in elevation.
Distinguishing Features:	This is a small species, reaching a maximum of about 1.5 in (38 mm) snout-vent length. It is dull colored, the dorsum greenish brown to brown, with orange-brown coloration on the dorsal surface of the limbs. Superficially, the tungara frog is toad like, with a very warty appearance, but unlike members of the genus *Bufo*, enlarged parotoid glands are absent. The fingers and toes are not webbed and the digits are not expanded to form disks.

Habitat/
Habits:

The tungara frog appears to be restricted to the Semi-evergreen Seasonal Forest formation in Belize, where it is generally found in semi-open and disturbed situations. It may also inhabit the Savanna formation, but its presence there has yet to be documented. They are primarily nocturnal, although some may be active on the forest floor in the rainy season. In some parts of the range, the tungara frog may aestivate during the dry season, and it is possible that this behavior may also occur in Belize. The call consists of two parts, the first a "whine," which may be followed by a "chuck," as two or more males start to call.

Breeding:

This species may utilize any calm body of water, from a small rain puddle to a permanent pond for breeding purposes. During amplexus, the females release the eggs and a jelly, which is whipped into a froth by the fertilizing male. This foam nest floats upon the surface of the water, with the eggs hatching in about 2 days. Tadpoles metamorphose in 4 to 5 weeks. Although the species may call throughout the rainy season, the most intensive breeding period is initiated by the first heavy rains of the season, usually in early to mid June in northern Belize.

Remarks:

The common name "tungara frog," utilized in parts of the species' range, is an approximation of the combined "whine" and "chuck" notes of the calling males.

WILLIAM DUELLMAN

GULF CHIRPING FROG
Syrrhophus leprus Cope

Range:	Low elevations of the Atlantic versant from Veracruz, Mexico, to Guatemala and Belize.
Distribution:	Known from the Orange Walk and Toledo Districts, but probably also occurs in the Cayo and Stann Creek Districts.
Distinguishing Features:	This is a small frog with a maximum snout-vent length of no more than 1.5 in (38 mm). Dorsal ground color ranges from yellowish green to tan, with darker reticulations or discrete spots. The body has a flattened appearance, with a large head and prominent eyes. The skin of the dorsum and upper limbs is smooth, the fingers and toes are not webbed, and the fingers and toes are slightly dilated to form disks.
Habitat/ Habits:	The gulf chirping frog is very poorly known in Belize, but appears to be an inhabitant of the Evergreen Broadleaf Forest and Semi-evergreen Seasonal Forest formations, where it has been found at elevations up to about 700 ft

(235 m). They are strictly nocturnal, and may be heard calling from low vegetation and dense thickets, especially during light rains. During the daylight, they probably take refuge under logs, rocks, and in crevices. The call is a birdlike "chirp," or "trink," repeated at erratic intervals.

Breeding: Eggs are deposited under debris on the ground, and hatch directly into small froglets. The breeding season is unknown in Belize, but it probably occurs during the rainy season, at least in the north.

Remarks: This small frog is considered by some herpetologists to belong to the genus *Eleutherodactylus*.

CAROL FARNETI FOSTER

ELEGANT NARROWMOUTH FROG
Gastrophryne elegans (Boulenger)

Range:	Low and elevations of the Atlantic versant from Veracruz, Mexico, to Honduras.
Distribution:	Apparently countrywide at low elevations.
Distinguishing Features:	This is a small frog, not exceeding 1.5 in (38 mm) snout-vent length, with a very small pointed head. There is a fold of skin across the back of the head, a character shared only with *Hypopachus variolosus* in Belize. It can be distinguished from the latter by the presence of only an inner metatarsal tubercle in *Gastrophryne*, as opposed to inner and outer tubercles in *Hypopachus*. The dorsal ground color is blackish brown, with gold-colored blotches on both the dorsum and upper surfaces of the limbs. The sides are black with scattered small white spots.
Habitat/ Habits:	So far, the narrowmouth toad is known only from four locations in the Orange Walk, Belize, Stann Creek, and Toledo Districts, although it probably will also be discovered in the other districts. Specimens are known from the

Evergreen Broadleaf Forest, Semi-evergreen Seasonal Forest, and Savanna vegetation formations, although the species' habitat preferences are as yet unclear. As with other members of the genus, these frogs probably prey upon ants, termites, and other small insects. They are fossorial, hiding under logs, rocks, and other debris, or digging into the soil. The call is high pitched, almost like the buzzing of an insect.

Breeding: This species has never been reported breeding in Belize, but it presumably does so at the onset of heavy rains in May or June. The males probably call from flooded ditches and pools, where the eggs are laid on the surface of the water to hatch in a few days time. The tadpoles probably metamorphose in 3 to 4 weeks.

Remarks: This enigmatic frog does not appear to be commonly encountered anywhere in Central America and has been reported only four times from Belize.

JOHN MEYER

SHEEP FROG
Hypopachus variolosus (Cope)

Range:	Low and moderate elevations from southern Texas on the Atlantic versant and Sinaloa, Mexico, on the Pacific to Costa Rica.
Distribution:	The sheep frog is known for certain from the Corozal, Orange Walk, Belize, Stann Creek, and Cayo Districts. Its presence in the wetter Toledo District has not yet been established.
Distinguishing Features:	Slightly larger than the narrowmouth frog, this species may reach 1.75 in (45 mm) snout-vent length. The dorsum is grey-brown to orange- brown in color, with a few scattered black markings, especially posteriorly. The sides and inguinal region are mottled with black and white, and there is a white stripe from the eye extending posteriorly to the throat. There is a fine mid-dorsal light line, and usually a mid-ventral light line with accessory lateral extensions. The head is small and pointed, with a fold of skin behind the head. This species differs from *Gastrophryne*

elegans in having two metatarsal tubercles rather than one and in its slightly larger size.

Habitat/
Habits:
The sheep frog seems to be an inhabitant of the Semi-evergreen Seasonal Forest formation and the marginal Evergreen Broadleaf Forest formation in Belize; it appears to prefer the open, edge, or disturbed situations within the forest. It has been found as high as 700 ft (233 m) in the country, although elsewhere in Central America it can be found above 3,000 ft (1000 m). This species is fossorial, hiding beneath logs, rocks, and other debris during the daytime. At night, particularly during the rainy season, they may venture forth to search for ants, termites, and other small insects. The call of the males is a sheep like bleat that may last 2 or 3 seconds.

Breeding:
This species breeds in northern Belize following initiation of the rainy season, and it is most likely to be actively calling following very heavy downpours. It may breed throughout the season, as late as October under the right conditions. Eggs are deposited in temporary situations, such as ponds and ditches, where they float in rafts on the surface. The eggs hatch in as little as 24 hours and meta-morphose into froglets in about 3 to 4 weeks.

Remarks:
Although this frog is known from the drier forests of Guatemala and Honduras to the south, it has not been found in the wetter parts of southern Belize.

CAROL FARNETI FOSTER

MEXICAN GLASS FROG
Hyalinobatrachium fleischmanni (Boettger)

Range:	Low and moderate elevations from Veracruz, Mexico, on the Atlantic versant and Guerrero, Mexico, on the Pacific to South America. *Distribution*: Known from about 200 to 1,600 ft (67 to 560 m) in elevation in the Cayo, Belize, and Toledo Districts, but probably also to be found in the Stann Creek District. Presumably also occurs at higher elevations in these districts.
Distinguishing Features:	The glass frog, with its small size of 1.25 in (32 mm) or less, light green color, and transparent ventral surface, is unlikely to be confused with any other frog in Belize. The toes are webbed and the tips are expanded as disks.
Habitat/ Habits:	It is found in the Evergreen Broadleaf Forest and Mountain Pine Ridge, and possibly the Subtropical Evergreen Forest formations. In the Mountain Pine Ridge, they are confined to the broadleaf forests that border the streams through the pine forests. Frequently encountered along

clear streams where they breed, Mexican glass frogs probably also inhabit epiphytes, such as bromeliads, in trees away from the streams in the more humid situations. Although successful breeding requires the presence of water in the streams, individuals may sometimes be found calling along dry streambeds in apparent anticipation of rains and ensuing water in the streams. They are nocturnal, and the call of the males is a bird-like "peep," usually vocalized in a chorus of many males along a stream.

Breeding: Breeding always takes place along clear streams, where the males vocalize from the vegetation overhanging the water. The eggs are deposited on the undersides, and occasionally the upper sides, of low vegetation, such as heliconias. The egg clutches are often attended by the males, who may wet them during dry periods. The eggs hatch in 1 to 3 weeks, depending upon environmental conditions, and the tadpoles fall into the streams. The tadpoles burrow into the stream detritus or the mud along the stream banks to complete their development, which may require several months. In Belize, the breeding season most likely coincides with the rainy season, although calling males have been observed in March in the southern Maya Mountains.

Remarks: Until recently, this frog was put in the genus *Centrolenella*, which is now considered to be a synonym of *Hyalinobatrachium*.

JOHN MEYER

RED-EYED TREEFROG
Agalychnis callidryas (Cope)

Range:	Low and moderate elevations from Veracruz, Mexico, to Panama on the Atlantic versant and Nicaragua to Panama on the Pacific.
Distribution:	Countrywide from sea level to at least 1,560 ft (520 m) in elevation.
Distinguishing Features:	This is a medium-sized frog, up to about 2.5 in (65 mm) snout-vent length. With its combination of bright green dorsal color, red eyes, and flanks barred with blue, it can be mistaken for no other Belizean frog. The feet are generally orangish in color and the tips of the digits expanded to form disks. The fingers are about one-half webbed, while the toes are about two-thirds webbed.
Habitat/ Habits:	The red-eyed treefrog is common during the rainy season around pools and water-filled ditches, where they are within or adjacent to the forest. They appear to be restricted to the Semi-evergreen Seasonal Forest and Evergreen Broadleaf Forest formations, although they may

also occur in the Subtropical Evergreen Forest formation. During the dry season, they apparently retreat to epiphytic bromeliads and other arboreal shelters, especially in the drier north. They are nocturnal and probably search for insects among the leaves and branches of the forest trees. The call of the male is usually a single note "cluck" or "chock," uttered at spaced intervals.

Breeding: This species congregates during the rainy season around the edges of forest pools and ditches, where the eggs are encased in a pale green jelly and deposited on the surface of leaves and vines overhanging the water. The eggs hatch within a week, and the tadpoles fall into the water where development into froglets requires about 2 months. Most breeding probably takes place early in the rainy season, but calling males have been heard as late as December in the north.

Remarks: This relatively common treefrog is extremely popular with photographers because of its outstanding appearance and the ease with which it may be photographed.

LOUISE EMMONS

MORELET'S TREEFROG
Agalychnis moreletii (Dumeril)

Range:	Moderate elevations from Veracruz, Mexico, to Honduras on the Atlantic versant and Guerrero, Mexico, to El Salvador on the Pacific.
Distribution:	Known only from about 1500 to 2,000 ft (500 to 667 m) in elevation in the Maya Mountains. It may occur at higher elevations if breeding sites are available.
Distinguishing Features:	This treefrog is similar in size and general appearance to *Agalychnis callidryas*, from which it differs in lacking the bright red eyes and barred blue markings on the flanks. Like *A. callidryas*, this species sometimes has white flecks on the dorsal surface, which is pale to dark green. The hands and feet are about three-fourths webbed.
Habitat/ Habits:	This species appears to replace *A. callidryas* at higher elevations in Belize, although the two have been found together at some localities. It appears to be restricted to the Evergreen Broadleaf Forest and Subtropical Evergreen Forest formations, where it probably inhabits the epi-

phytes, fronds, and branches of the forest trees. It has been found in Cayo and Toledo Districts, but undoubtedly also occurs in appropriate habitats in the Stann Creek District. The call has been described as a single "wor-or-orp," repeated at varying intervals.

Breeding: Morelet's treefrog breeds in forest pools, where the eggs are deposited on vegetation overhanging the water. The eggs are in a gelatinous matrix, and there appears to be about twice the number of an *A. callidryas* egg mass. The tadpoles fall into the water upon hatching, and development probably takes at least 2 months. As these frogs probably depend upon temporary pools for breeding, most activity probably takes place early in the rainy season, during the months of June, July, and August in Belize.

Remarks: Although this species has been reported only a few times from Belize, it is probably widespread throughout the Maya Mountains, wherever proper habitat conditions are met.

JONATHAN CAMPBELL

BROMELIAD TREEFROG
Hyla bromeliacia Schmidt

Range:	Moderate elevations of the Atlantic versant in Belize, Guatemala, and Honduras.
Distribution:	Known only from about 2,000 ft (667 m) in the Maya Mountains in the Toledo District.
Distinguishing Features:	This is a small frog, with a maximum snout-vent length of 1.25 in (32 mm). It is a pale brown or yellowish tan species, with no distinctive dark markings on the dorsum, although a few whitish or dark flecks may be present. It may be distinguished from *Hyla picta* by the presence in *Hyla picta* of a white dorsolateral stripe bordered below by a brown stripe, and from *Hyla microcephala* by the presence of distinct dark markings on the dorsum in *H. microcephala*. The tips of the fingers and toes are expanded to form disks, and the toes are about two-thirds webbed.
Habitat/ Habits:	This small arboreal frog is restricted to the Subtropical Evergreen Forest formation in Belize, where it presum-

ably inhabits the epiphytic bromeliads on the forest trees. The single specimen known from Belize was found on a shrub about 5 ft (1.67 m) above ground at night at Gloria Spring in the Columbia River Forest Reserve. The call is a soft insectlike chirp of five or six notes, repeated at infrequent intervals.

Breeding: In other parts of its range, the bromeliad treefrog deposits its eggs in water in epiphytic bromeliads. Clutches of about 12 to 15 eggs appear to be normal, and the tadpoles undergo their development in the bromeliads. It probably breeds throughout the year if sufficient moisture is present.

Remarks: In Guatemala and Honduras, this species is an inhabitant of the wet forests between 2,000 and 5,000 ft (667 and 1,667 m) in elevation. Its recent discovery in Belize indicates that the wet forests of the southern Maya Mountains share their biological history with the nearby mountains of Guatemala and Honduras.

CAROL FARNETI FOSTER

VARIEGATED TREEFROG
Hyla ebraccata Cope

Range:	Low and moderate elevations from Veracruz, Mexico, to Panama on the Atlantic versant and Costa Rica to Columbia on the Pacific.
Distribution:	Known from about 300 to 1,200 ft (100 to 400 m) in the Orange Walk, Cayo, and Stann Creek Districts, but probably also to be found in the other districts.
Distinguishing Features:	This is a small treefrog, with a maximum snout-vent length of about 1.5 in (36 mm). The dorsal pattern is variable, with a ground color of cream to yellow and dark brown hourglass-shaped markings, bars, or spots. In a few individuals, there are no dorsal markings. A distinct axillary web is present, and there are no dorsolateral white lines. The tips of the digits are expanded to form disks and the fingers are about one-half webbed and the toes about three-fourths webbed. Patternless individuals may be distinguished from *Hyla loquax* by the orange-red coloration of the webbing and posterior thighs in the latter.

Habitat/
Habits:

This species appears to be restricted to the Semi-evergreen Seasonal Forest formation, and possibly the drier portions of the Evergreen Broadleaf Forest formation. During the rainy season, these small treefrogs can be found around pools of water in or at the edge of the forest. They are nocturnal, and presumably spend most of their nonbreeding time up in the forest trees, possibly in bromeliads. The call is a high-pitched "squawk" or "creeek" repeated at frequent intervals.

Breeding:

Variegated treefrogs congregate around forest pools following the start of the rainy season and may continue to breed until as late as October. Calling males are usually found on grasses and low branches overhanging the water, and the eggs are deposited on the surface of leaves, usually of herbaceous plants, above the water. Following hatching, the tadpoles fall into the pool to complete their development, which requires 4 to 6 weeks.

Remarks:

Although common in the forests of northern and central Belize, the variegated treefrog has yet to be found in the wetter south. Future studies in the Toledo District are needed to determine its presence or absence there.

CAROL FARNETI FOSTER

RED-FOOTED TREEFROG
Hyla loquax Gaige and Stuart

Range:	Low and moderate elevations of the Atlantic versant from Veracruz, Mexico, to Costa Rica.
Distribution:	Found throughout the country from sea level to about 1,000 ft (333 m) in elevation.
Distinguishing Features:	A medium-sized treefrog, reaching a snout-vent length of about 2 in (50 mm). These frogs may be distinguished by the presence of a prominent axillary membrane and the orange to red coloration of the hands, feet, and thighs. The dorsal coloration at night is usually tan, with scattered dark markings, but the daytime coloration may vary from light brown to cream, especially on individuals located in the sunlight. The fingers are about two-thirds webbed and the toes are nearly fully webbed; the tips of the digits are expanded to form disks.
Habitat/ Habits:	Red-footed treefrogs are found during the rainy season in and around temporary and permanent pools in the forests and in the savannas. Occurrence in the savannas appears

to be limited to pools with "islands" or hammocks of broadleaf forest nearby. During the dry season, individuals may be heard calling infrequently from medium heights in forest trees, especially at dawn and dusk. The call has been described as a "hah-onk," repeated at frequent intervals.

Breeding: Frequent vocalization is initiated by the onset of the rainy season, but in Belize it appears that breeding is delayed until well into the season. Vocalization around breeding sites may continue on into late October in some areas. The eggs are deposited in or immediately above the water, usually attached to aquatic vegetation. The tadpoles, which are wary and prefer deeper water, develop into froglets after 4 to 6 weeks.

CAROL FARNETI FOSTER

YELLOW TREEFROG
Hyla microcephala Cope

Range:	Low and moderate elevations from Veracruz, Mexico, to Honduras and from Panama to Venezuela on the Atlantic versant and from Honduras to Panama on the Pacific.
Distribution:	Found throughout the country from sea level to at least 1,000 ft (333 m) in elevation. Its distribution in the Maya Mountains is not well known, and the species may occur at higher elevations.
Distinguishing Features:	This is a small treefrog, with a maximum snout-vent length of 1.5 in (38 mm). The dorsal ground color varies from pale yellow or light brown at night to a reddish tan to medium brown during the daytime. The dorsal color is broken by irregular dark spots, reticulations, or an X-shaped mark in the scapular area. There is sometimes a dark line extending posteriorly along the side from the tympanum, but this is almost never accompanied by a bold light stripe extending to the groin as in *Hyla picta*, with which it might be confused. The latter never exhibits

the bold dark X-shaped dorsal markings characteristic of *microcephala*. The tips of the digits are expanded to form disks, and the toes are about three-fourths webbed.

Habitat/
Habits:
The yellow treefrog is known from most of the vegetation formations in Belize, except for the Subtropical Evergreen Forest and Elfin Forest formations. It appears to be most abundant in open or disturbed areas, shying away from the deep forest. These small treefrogs are generally encountered around standing water, ranging from temporary ditches and pools to permanent lagoons. They appear to be inhabitants of the lower parts of vegetation and are seldom heard calling from any great height in the trees. The call is a rapid cricketlike sound, "skreek, skreek, skreek," repeated at frequent intervals.

Breeding:
Although most breeding probably takes place during the rainy season, males of the common treefrog may be heard calling from flooded areas anytime during the year following appreciable rainfall. Males call from grass and low bushes in and around the water, and the eggs are deposited in small masses attached to emergent vegetation at the surface of the water. Tadpoles probably complete their development in about two months.

LOUISE EMMONS

MOUNTAIN FRINGE-LIMBED FROG
Hyla minera Wilson, McCranie, and Williams

Range:	Known only from the Maya Mountains of Belize and the mountains of the Department of Baja Verapaz, Guatemala.
Distribution:	Currently known only from the Columbia River Forest in the southern Maya Mountains.
Distinguishing Features:	This is a large treefrog, reaching a maximum snout-vent length of about 3.5 in (89 mm). This distinctive frog has a dark and medium brown mottled dorsum, covered with tubercles. The fingers and toes are well webbed, with expanded disks, and the sides of the limbs are fringed with dermal projections. In males, the prepollex is armed with black sharp-tipped spines. The skin of the head is co-ossified with the skull, and the iris is gold with brown reticulations.
Habitat/ Habits:	The mountain fringe-limbed frog is an inhabitant of the Subtropical Evergreen Forest formation, where a single individual was found on a palm frond about 10 ft (3.3 m)

above ground at night. Elsewhere in its range it has been found in arboreal bromeliads, and on low branches and logs. Nothing is known regarding vocalization in this species.

Breeding: Nothing is known regarding the breeding biology of this species, but the closely related *Hyla salvaje* from Honduras is known to deposit its eggs in water-filled tree cavities, where the eggs and tadpoles appear to be guarded by the males. The tadpoles apparently feed on eggs of their own species.

Remarks: This recently described species is known only from Gloria Spring in the Columbia River Forest Reserve. This small area in the southwest corner of the Maya Mountains exhibits a close relationship to the montane areas of nearby Guatemala and Honduras, and appears to be unique for Belize. The future of *Hyla minera* and the rest of this montane fauna and flora in Belize rests with the protection of this unique habitat.

CAROL FARNETI FOSTER

CRICKET TREEFROG
Hyla picta (Gunther)

Range: Low elevations of the Atlantic versant from San Luis Po-
                  tosi, Mexico, to northern Honduras.

Distribution: Probably countrywide from sea level to at least 1,000 ft
                  (333 m) in elevation. The upper limits of its distribution in
                  the Maya Mountains is unknown.

Distinguishing This is the smallest of the Belizean treefrogs, with a maxi-
Features: mum snout-vent length of about 1 in (25 mm). The dorsal
                  color of the cricket treefrog varies from a cream color to a
                  medium olive-brown, and there may be scattered dark
                  spots on the dorsum. The most conspicuous feature is a
                  white stripe extending from the nostril posteriorly to the
                  groin region, often accompanied by a dark stripe below.
                  This is the only Belizean frog that consistently exhibits this
                  light dorsolateral light stripe. *Hyla microcephala*, which
                  may occasionally show a light dorsolateral stripe, differs
                  from *picta* in having bold dark dorsal markings. The tips

of the digits are expanded to form disks, and the toes are about three-fourths webbed.

Habitat/
Habits:

The cricket treefrog is known from the Evergreen Broadleaf Forest, Semi-evergreen Seasonal Forest, Mountain Pine Ridge, Karst Hills Forest, and Savanna vegetation formations, as well as the Coastal Lagoons and Marshes and Interior Wetlands formations. In the more open formations, they appear to be restricted to situations with forest vegetation. Although they occur near the ground around water in the rainy season, during the dry season they may be heard calling from high up in trees, particularly at dawn and dusk. The male's call is a shrill, cricket-like "creek, creek," repeated frequently.

Breeding:

Following the start of the rainy season, these small frogs congregate around ponds and ditches where the males call from grass, bushes, and trees in or around the water. The eggs are deposited on vegetation in or just above the water, where the tadpoles undergo development that requires 6 to 8 weeks.

CAROL FARNETI FOSTER

PEPPER TREEFROG
Phrynohyas venulosa (Laurenti)

Range: Low and moderate elevations from Tamaulipas, Mexico, to Costa Rica on the Atlantic versant and from Sinaloa, Mexico, to Panama on the Pacific.

Distribution: Occurs at the lower elevations throughout Belize.

Distinguishing Features: This is the largest of the Belizean treefrogs, reaching a snout-vent length of about 4 in (102 mm). The dorsal color is a mottling of cream to tan and medium to dark brown. The skin is very glandular, with numerous raised pustules. The tips of the digits are greatly expanded to form disks and the toes are about three-fourths webbed. Prominent eyes are strikingly marked with a gold iris with dark reticulations. They lack vertical bars on the lips and the cream and black mottling on the flanks, characteristic of *Smilisca baudinii* with which they might be confused. When handled, these frogs release a sticky secretion that is difficult to remove and may prove irritating to the human skin and the eyes.

Habitat/
Habits:

The pepper treefrog is known from the Evergreen Broad-leaf Forest, Semi-evergreen Forest, Mountain Pine Ridge, Karst Hills Forest, Savanna, and Coastal Lagoon and Marsh formations. In the more heavily forested formations, it appears to be restricted to disturbed and edge situations. It may be heard calling from high in forest trees during the dry season, and it is frequently encountered around houses and buildings, particularly near water sources. A common retreat during the dry season appears to be bromeliads, which retain moisture and protect the frogs from the sun's rays. They may also retreat to tree holes, under tree bark, and in the protected parts of banana and heliconia leaves. The call is a loud, nasal "grawl," which may be repeated frequently.

Breeding:

Although this species may vocalize during the dry season, breeding appears to be limited to the rainy season. Following heavy rains, choruses of males may congregate around temporary pools and ditches, where the eggs are laid in the water and spread over the surface in a film. Development of the tadpoles probably requires 5 to 6 weeks.

Remarks:

The common name "pepper treefrog" is in allusion to the sneezing effect that may be elicited by exposure to this frog's skin secretions. These secretions probably serve a protective function against predators and may also protect the skin against desiccation.

CAROL FARNETI FOSTER

STAUFFER'S TREEFROG
Scinax staufferi (Cope)

Range:	Low and moderate elevations from Tamaulipas, Mexico, to Panama on the Atlantic versant and from Guerrero, Mexico, to Panama on the Pacific.
Distribution:	Widespread at lower elevations.
Distinguishing Features:	This is a small species, reaching a maximum snout-vent length of about 1.25 in (38 mm). Compared with the other Belizean treefrogs, this appears to be an elongated species, due in part to the pronounced snout that overhangs the lower jaw. The dorsal ground color is tan to light grey-brown, with several darker stripes or elongated spots. The dorsum is slightly warty, as are the upper limb surfaces. The fingers are without webs and the toes are about two-thirds webbed; the tips of the digits are expanded to form disks.
Habitat/ Habits:	Stauffer's treefrog is known from all of the vegetation formations in Belize except the Subtropical Evergreen Forest and Elfin Forest formations. It appears to be absent

from the deep forest in those heavily vegetated formations and is a common inhabitant of the savannas, open forests, and disturbed situations. During the dry season, these frogs are frequently found in bromeliads, rolled heliconia and banana leaves, and in houses and other buildings. Calling by the males may take place infrequently during the dry season, especially at dawn and dusk. The call has been described as a "whark," "braaa," or a series of short, nasal notes "ah-ah-ah-ah."

Breeding: Stauffer's treefrogs seem to be among the earliest breeders in Belize, forming choruses following the first heavy rains. The males call from low vegetation, particularly grasses and palmetto fronds in the water. The eggs are deposited in small clumps in temporary and permanent ponds, ditches, and marshy areas, where the tadpoles seek refuge among the aquatic vegetation while undergoing development.

Remarks: Along with *Smilisca baudinii*, this species is one of the most frequently encountered frogs in populated areas. During the dry season, they often invade houses to search for insects and to evade the desiccating heat. In the older literature, this species was considered to be a member of the genus *Hyla*, and more recently, *Ololygon*, which has since been synonymized with *Scinax*.

JOHN MEYER

MEXICAN TREEFROG
Smilisca baudinii (Dumeril and Bibron)

Range:	Low, moderate, and intermediate elevations from southern Texas on the Atlantic versant and southern Sonora, Mexico, on the Pacific to Costa Rica.
Distribution:	Countrywide at the lower elevations. The extent of its distribution in the Maya Mountains is poorly known at this time.
Distinguishing Features:	Along with *Phrynohyas venulosa*, this is one of the largest treefrogs in Belize, reaching a snout-vent length of about 2.75 in (70 mm). It may be distinguished from *P. venulosa* by its smoother skin and lack of sticky glandular secretions. It differs from other treefrogs, except *Phrynohyas venulosa* and *Smilisca cyanosticta*, in its larger size and paired vocal sacs in males. From the related *Smilisca cyanosticta* in may be distinguished by the dark-bordered white lip stripe and spotted posterior thighs in *cyanosticta*. The Mexican treefrog is variable in color and pattern, but there is usually a ground color of tan to green,

interrupted by various dorsal dark blotches. There is a dark line running from the eye posteriorly to the region of the upper arm, and the upper lip is usually barred. The toes are about three-fourths webbed, and the tips of the digits are expanded to form disks.

Habitat/ Habits: The Mexican treefrog is known from all of the vegetation formations in Belize, except the Subtropical Evergreen Forest and Elfin Forest formations. In the heavily forested areas, it is frequently encountered in open, edge, or otherwise disturbed situations, especially during the rainy season. During the dry season, they probably retreat to the forest, where they may inhabit bromeliads, loose tree bark, and other protected hiding places. They may also be found in rolled heliconia and banana leaves, and around buildings that offer protective shelter. Their call, a nasal "wank, wank, wank" is repeated frequently during breeding choruses and may also be heard occasionally during the dry season.

Breeding: Breeding is initiated with the arrival of heavy rains in June and July and may continue until October or November in some areas. The eggs are deposited as a surface film in still water, usually temporary ponds and ditches, where the tadpoles undergo development that requires about 2 to 3 months.

Remarks: The Mexican treefrog is one of the most common anurans in Belize, and one which is likely to be encountered in populated areas, including Belize City.

LOUISE EMMONS

BLUE-SPOTTED TREEFROG
Smilisca cyanosticta (Smith)

Range: Low and moderate elevations of the Atlantic versant from Veracruz, Mexico, to Guatemala and Belize.

Distribution: Known only from between 500 and 2,000 ft (167 and 667 m) in the Maya Mountains.

Distinguishing Features: This is another relatively large Belizean treefrog, reaching a snout-vent length of about 2.5 in (64 mm). The dorsal ground color is pale green or tan with olive green or dark brown markings, and the upper lip is silvery or creamy white. This species may be distinguished from *Smilisca baudinii* by its light lip stripe and the blue spotting on the posterior thighs. It differs from *Hyla minera* in lacking the dermal fringes on the limbs and in lacking dorsal tubercles. It can be distinguished from sympatric *Eleutherodactylus* by its enlarged toe disks and extensive toe webbing and from members of the genus *Rana* by the enlarged finger and toe disks.

Habitat/
Habits:

The blue-spotted treefrog is currently known from the Evergreen Broadleaf Forest and Subtropical Evergreen Forest formations, but its actual distribution in Belize is poorly documented. It appears to occur in the high forests, probably inhabiting arboreal bromeliads and trees at low to medium heights. The call has been described as one or two short notes, "wonk, wonk."

Breeding:

This species has been found breeding in July in the Chiquibul National Park, where males were vocalizing along water-filled vehicle tracks through the forest. Another large breeding chorus was documented during the rainy season in the Cockscomb Basin. Eggs have been found scattered on the surface of temporary ponds, and in other parts of its range it has been found to deposit eggs in water-filled depressions in logs, forks of tree trunks, and in springs and quiet stream pools. Development of the tadpoles probably requires 6 to 8 weeks.

CAROL FARNETI FOSTER

CASQUEHEAD TREEFROG
Triprion petasatus (Cope)

Range:	Low and moderate elevations of the Atlantic versant from Yucatan, Mexico, to Guatemala and Honduras.
Distribution:	Found from near sea level to about 700 ft (233 m) in elevation in northern and central Belize.
Distinguishing Features:	This is another relatively large treefrog, with adults reaching about 2.5 in (64 mm) snout-vent length. With its bony, projecting snout, the casquehead treefrog can be confused with no other species in Belize. The dorsal ground color is tan to olive green with brown or black spots and blotches, a pattern that continues onto the upper limb surfaces. The overall effect may be that of lichen-encrusted tree bark. The fingers have only rudimentary webbing, and the toes are about two-thirds webbed; the tips of the digits are expanded to form disks.
Habitat/ Habits:	The casquehead treefrog is known only from the drier forest formations in the northern and central parts of Belize. They are known from the Semi-evergreen Seasonal

Forest formation in the north and the marginal Evergreen Broadleaf Forest formation along the Hummingbird Highway near Blue Hole National Park. Except during their brief breeding season, these frogs are rarely encountered, apparently inhabiting tree holes above ground. The bony, expanded head is used to plug tree holes where these frogs retreat, possibly as protection against predation or desiccation. The call has been described as a ducklike "quack."

Breeding: This species breeds following the first heavy downpours of the rainy season, as soon as the temporary pools are filled with water. Large choruses of calling males may congregate in one location, with breeding lasting up to about a week. The adults disappear as soon as breeding terminates, and the eggs and subsequent tadpoles undergo development in the temporary pools.

Remarks: Although this species is known from Honduras, its preference for drier habitats probably precludes its occurrence in the wet southern third of Belize.

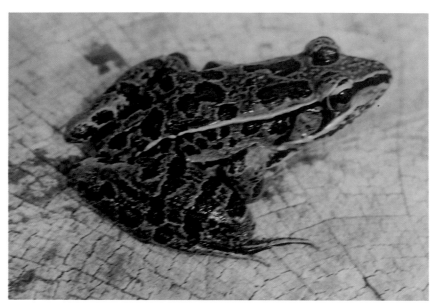

JOHN MEYER

RIO GRANDE LEOPARD FROG
Rana berlandieri Baird

Range:	Low, moderate, and intermediate elevations of the Atlantic versant from Texas to Nicaragua.
Distribution:	Widespread at the lower elevations. The distribution of the species in the Maya Mountains is poorly known.
Distinguishing Features:	A large frog, with a maximum snout-vent length of about 4.5 in (114 mm). The dorsal ground color is tan to greenish brown, with scattered large dark spots. Dorsolateral ridges, often edged with white to yellow, are present. The tips of the digits are not expanded, and the feet are strongly webbed.
Habitat/ Habits:	The Rio Grande leopard frog is known from all of the vegetation formations except the Subtropical Evergreen Forest and Elfin Forest formations. The species has been found from sea level to about 1,000 ft (333 m) in elevation and may occur at higher elevations in the Maya Mountains. These frogs are almost always encountered at night near water, usually permanent or temporary ponds, marshes,

or slow-moving streams. During dry periods they may bury themselves under logs, rocks, or other forest debris. The call is described as a rapid, low-pitched trill.

Breeding: Most breeding appears to take place during the rainy season, although the species may be heard calling at other times. The eggs are laid in still water, where the tadpoles undergo development for several months.

COURTNEY CONWAY

MAYA MOUNTAINS FROG
Rana juliani Hillis and De Sa

Range: Maya Mountains of Belize

Distribution: Known from between about 1,000 and 3,000 ft (333 and 1,000 m) in the Maya Mountains in the Cayo and Toledo Districts. Probably also occurs in the Stann Creek District.

Distinguishing Features: This is a large frog, reaching about 4 in (102 mm) in snout-vent length. The dorsal ground color is medium brown, with scattered dark brown markings. There are dorso-lateral ridges extending to the groin, and the sides are distinctly darker than the dorsum. The tympanum is about equal in diameter to the eye, and there is a dark face mask and light stripe on the upper jaw. The toes are fully webbed, and the tips of the digits are not expanded. Vocal slits and sacs are absent in males.

Habitat/ Habits: This species is known from the Subtropical Evergreen Forest and Mountain Pine Ridge formations and probably also occurs in the Evergreen Broadleaf Forest formation.

These frogs appear to be restricted to the environs of streams in the mountains.

Breeding: No vocalizations are known for this species and, given the absence of vocal slits or sacs, it is unlikely that there are any breeding calls. Tadpoles have been found in streams, and presumably eggs are laid in them. The breeding season is not known for certain, but some streams where individuals have been found are known to dry out in the dry season. It is therefore likely that breeding takes place early in the rainy season.

Remarks: The Maya Mountains frog was named for Julian Lee, a herpetologist who has done much to advance our knowledge of the Belizean herpetofauna. The type locality of this species is Little Quartz Ridge in the Toledo District.

JACOB MARLIN

RAINFOREST FROG
Rana vaillanti Brocchi

Range: Low and moderate elevations of both versants from Vera-
                  cruz and Chiapas, Mexico, to Panama.

Distribution: Countrywide from near sea level to at least 2,000 ft (667
                  m) in elevation.

Distinguishing This is the largest frog in Belize, with a maximum snout-
Features: vent length of about 5 in (127 mm), and it is second in size
                  only to *Bufo marinus* among the anurans. The dorsal
                  ground color is a brownish to bronze posteriorly, with
                  varying amounts of green anteriorly, especially on the
                  head and shoulders. There are dorsolateral ridges and
                  raised glandular ridges on the thighs. There is neither a
                  dark face mask nor a light line along the upper lip as in
                  Rana juliani.

Habitat/   As its common name indicates, this species is often associ-
Habits: ated with the forested areas, where it is never found far
                  from streams or forest pools. It is known from the Ever-
                  green Broadleaf Forest, Semi-evergreen Seasonal Forest,

Karst Hills Forest, Interior Wetlands, Savanna, and Mountain Pine Ridge formations. In the latter two formations, it is only found along permanent streams. Although this frog is primarily nocturnal, it may be encountered during the daytime resting around the margin of forest pools and streams. The call has been described as "chuckling" or "grunts."

Breeding: Breeding probably takes place throughout the year, especially in the wetter southern part of the country. Eggs are deposited in forest pools or still sections of streams, where tadpoles undergo development for several months.

Remarks: In much of the literature, this frog was known as *Rana palmipes*, a species now considered to be restricted to South America. The type locality for *R. vaillanti* is thought to be the Mullins River in Belize.

CAROL FARNETI FOSTER

MEXICAN BURROWING FROG
Rhinophrynus dorsalis Dumeril and Bibron

Range:	Low elevations from southern Texas to Honduras on the Atlantic versant and Michoacan, Mexico, to Costa Rica on the Pacific.
Distribution:	Found at lower elevations throughout Belize wherever soil conditions permit this fossorial species to burrow. It has been reported from all the districts except Stann Creek, but probably also occurs there.
Distinguishing Features:	This frog, with its color, amorphous body shape, and small cone-shaped head, is unlike any other in Belize. The maximum snout-vent length is 2.75 in (70 mm), and the dorsal color is bluish black with a red mid-dorsal stripe and scattered red markings.
Habitat/ Habits:	This bizarre frog appears to be primarily an inhabitant of open or disturbed situations in the wetter parts of its range and elsewhere restricted to seasonal forests with a noticeable dry season. In Belize, it has been found in both open and forested situations in the north and in open and dis-

turbed habitats in the central and southern parts of the country. It is an accomplished burrower, spending the dry season underground and coming to the surface with the onset of the rainy season. During the wetter months these frogs may leave their burrows at night to forage for insects, particularly ants and termites, but their locomotion is relatively clumsy. Its call is a deep, drawn-out "wow" or "woah," which in chorus from a distance may sound like machinery.

Breeding: Most breeding activity takes place at the onset of the first heavy rains, after which temporary ponds, or aguadas, fill with water. The males begin to call from their underground burrows with the onset of thundershowers, although they may not make an appearance for several days if sufficient rain does not fall. When conditions are right, males and females congregate in large numbers at breeding ponds, where the males' combined vocalizations may be heard for more than a mile. Eggs are deposited singly and sink to the bottom, where they may later coalesce into clumps. The eggs hatch after a few days into schooling tadpoles that metamorphose into burrowing froglets after a length of time that is temperature dependent, but more or less synchronous for a clutch. In most situations, breeding congregations occur only once at the onset of the rainy season, but in central Belize near the Sibun River, breeding congregations were heard calling on six separate occasions between late June and early November in one year, always following heavy rains. It was subsequently discovered that this population was utilizing the floodplain of the river for breeding and was apparently stimulated by the combination of heavy rains and the flooding river.

Elfin Forest   John Hall

Semi-Evergreen Seasonal Forest
John R. Meyer

Subtropical Evergreen Forest
Louise Emmons

References

Campbell, J. and J. Vannini. 1989. Distribution of amphibians and reptiles in Guatemala and Belize. Proc. Western Foundation Vert. Zool. 4(1):1–21.

Campbell, J. Savage, and J. Meyer. 1994. A new species of *Eleutherodactylus* (Anura: Leptodactylidae) of the *rugulosus* group from Guatemala and Belize. Herpetologica 50(4): 412–419.

Duellman, W. 1970. The hylid frogs of Middle America. Monogr. Mus. Nat. Hist., Univ. Kansas, No. 1, 753 pp, 2 vols.

Duellman, W. 1993. Amphibian species of the world: additions and corrections. Univ. Kansas Mus. Nat. Hist. Spec. Publ. 21: 1–372.

Frost, D. 1985. Amphibian species of the world: a taxonomic and geographic reference. Allen Press, Inc., Lawrence, Kansas, 732 p.

Hartshorn, G., L. Nicolait, L. Hartshorn, G. Bevier, R. Brightman, J. Cal, A. Cawich, W. Davidson, R. Dubois, C. Dyer, J. Gibson, W. Hawley, J. Leonard, R. Nicolait, D. Weyer, H. White, and C. Wright. 1984. Belize: Country Environmental Profile: A field study. Robert Nicolait and Associates, Ltd., Belize City, Belize, 151 p.

Henderson, R. and L. Hoevers. 1975. A checklist and key to the amphibians and reptiles of Belize, Central America. Milwaukee Publ. Mus., Contrib. in Biol. and Geol. 5: 1–63.

Hillis, D. and R. De Sa. 1988. Phylogeny and taxonomy of the *Rana palmipes* group. Herpetol. Monogr. 2: 1–26.

Iremonger, S. and R. Sayre. 1994. Bladen Nature Reserve, Belize: Rapid Ecological Assessment. The Nature Conservancy, 77 p.

Lee, J. 1980. An ecogeographic analysis of the herpetofauna of the Yucatan Peninsula. Univ. Kansas Mus. Nat. Hist. Misc. Publ. 67: 1–75.

Liner, E. 1994. Scientific and common names for the amphibians and reptiles of Mexico in English and Spanish. Soc. for Study of Amph. and Rept., Herpetological Circular 23: 1–113.

McCoy, C. J. 1990. Additions to the herpetofauna of Belize, Central America. Caribbean J. of Sci. 26(3–4): 164–166.

Meerman, J. 1993. Checklist of the reptiles and amphibians of the Shipstern Nature Reserve. Occ. Pap. Belize Nat. Hist. Soc. 2(1–11): 65–69.

Mendelson, J. 1994. A new species of toad (Anura: Bufonidae) from the lowlands of eastern Guatemala. Occ. Pap. Mus. Nat. Hist., Univ. Kansas 166: 1–21.

Neill, W. 1965. New and noteworthy amphibians and reptiles from British Honduras. Bull. Florida State Mus. 9(3): 77–130.

Neill, W. and R. Allen. 1959. Studies on the amphibians and reptiles of British Honduras. Publ. Research Div., Ross Allen's Reptile Inst. 2(1): 1–76.

————. 1959. Additions to the British Honduras herpetofaunal list. Herpetologica 15(4): 235–240.

————. 1961. Further studies on the herpetology of British Honduras. Herpetologica 17(1): 37–52.

Parker, T., B. Holst, L. Emmons, and J. Meyer. 1993. A biological assessment of the Columbia River Forest Reserve, Toledo District, Belize. Conservation International RAP Working Papers 3: 1–81.

Russell, S. 1964. A distributional study of the birds of British Honduras. Ornithological Monogr. 1:1–195.

Schmidt, K. 1941. The amphibians and reptiles of British Honduras. Field Mus. Nat. Hist. Zool. Ser. 22(8): 475–510.

Stafford, P. 1994. Amphibians and reptiles of the Upper Raspaculo River Basin, Maya Mountains, Belize. British Herp. Soc. Bull. 47: 23–29.

Wright, A., D. Romney, R. Arbuckle, and E. Vial. 1959. Land in British Honduras. Colonial Res. Publ. 24.